MW00875224

Made in United States
Troutdale, OR
03/13/2024

18429837R00056